LESSONS FROM A Dragonfly

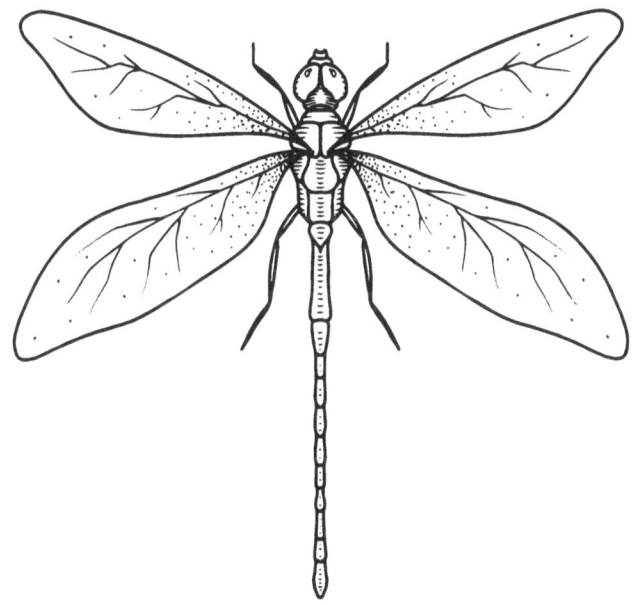

MAKAILA FAULKNER

Lessons From A Dragonfly
© Makaila Faulkner 2024

All rights reserved. No part of this publication may be reproduced, stored in a retrieval system, or transmitted in any form or by any means, electronic, mechanical, photocopying, recording or otherwise, without the prior written permission of the author.

ISBN: 978-1-923289-11-6(Paperback)

 A catalogue record for this work is available from the National Library of Australia

Cover Design: Makaila Faulkner and Clark & Mackay
Format and Typeset: Makaila Faulkner and Clark & Mackay
Published by Makaila Faulkner and Clark & Mackay
Proudly printed in Australia by Clark & Mackay

She said the thing about love, it's always pretty.
But what's the good in a flower if it doesn't grow?

— LEAVING FOR LONDON | PACIFIC AVENUE

INTRODUCTION

The dragonfly found me in the space in-between who I was and who I was meant to be. I was enduring a painful limbo; I was adjusting to a new life after I made the decision to leave my long-term partner. My new world was uncomfortable, and the unfamiliarity was terrifying.

I recall an otherwise insignificant day where I had three separate encounters with dragonflies. Two of them were dead and decaying upside-down on a warehouse floor. The sight of them caused me to momentarily wake from my current state of oblivion. I felt defeated looking at them. It felt like a waste to see them in this state, in some place where they did not belong. A part of me that felt like one of those dead dragonflies. There they were, alone, and rotting, and life continued around them as though they didn't exist.

That was the first time I remembered feeling anything at all following the breakdown of my life as I knew it. When I saw the third dragonfly, I was relieved to see that it was alive. It was on my passenger side window, and it sat with me in silence for a moment. I googled the symbolism behind a dragonfly and learned that they represent change, transformation, and self-realisation. How relevant, I thought to myself.

The title of this collection of poetry is inspired by the lessons that came from my own journey through change.

Writing has always been a hobby of mine, and during this time, it undoubtedly saved my life.

This collection discusses my experience of letting go of my first love, the questioning, the dismantling, the heartbreak, the grief, and finally, the acceptance.

The purpose of this collection was to help ease my own mind; I needed an escape and an outlet for the emotions and thoughts that were consuming me during this time.

If nothing else, my hope is that you can find a piece of yourself within these pages. And that in times of deep loneliness, I hope these words can remind you that although our journeys may differ, know that there is someone out there, that at some point in their life, walked a similar path, and felt the pain that you too, have felt.

And I hope that brings you some kind of comfort.

Makaila
x

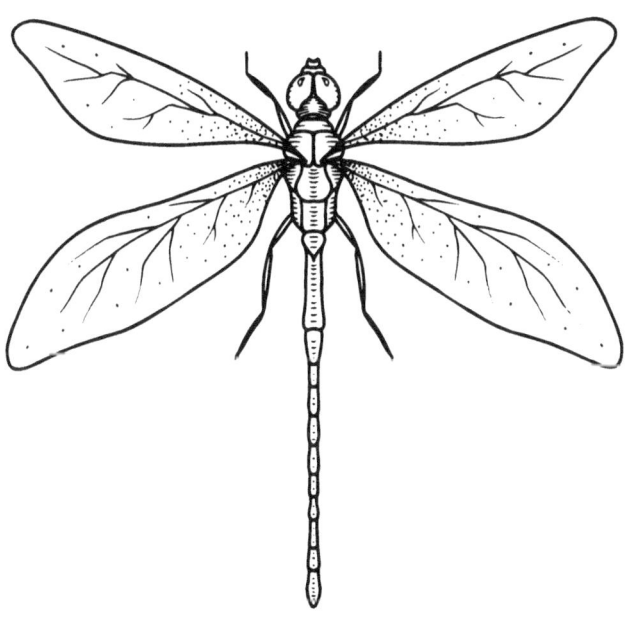

THE MEANING OF LOVE

I learned that it was never about completing each other,
Or about being each other's 'other half'.
For we are complete and enough on our own.
It's about enhancing each other,
And about embarking on a journey of infinite growth in order to find our way back home to ourselves.

UNTOUCHABLE

I can get caught up wishing I had the key that unlocks that glorious mind of yours.
What I would do to understand the pathways of your intriguing mind, and the way to your tender heart.
Tell me, what would I find?
I'm curious to understand how you made it here,
What lessons taught you to be this way,
To know what thoughts are truly your own,
And how all these things lead you to me.
I suppose that's the attraction with the untouchable.
You never get to fully know,
you never get to deeply understand,
It's a beautiful mystery,
and it's forever out of reach.

GRIEF

I have grieved the loss of time together,
the loss of intimacy,
and the loss of oneness we once shared.
But I am yet to mourn the life we built together.
And that may be the hardest part of all.
Watching our lives fall apart so effortlessly,
knowing that it was not caused by some enormous hurricane,
or an unwelcome earthquake.
It was not caused by infidelity,
or abuse.
It was caused by the growing of one heart,
that watched,
slowly,
As the other failed to keep up.

THE INEVITABLE

I can't look myself in the eye without seeing your innocence.
I know it'll break your heart,
but I know that you've broken mine a thousand times over.
This is the inevitable,
but I can't bring myself to accept it yet.
Our souls were meant to be one,
for that,
I am certain.
I simply didn't realize that it wasn't meant to last forever.

POTENTIAL

I've had a troubling realisation; *this isn't going to work*.
Parts of me are still trying to keep this disaster contained.
Perhaps if I can convince myself that it's a lie,
It might just disappear.
Maybe I can brush it off as just another intrusive thought.
Though, my attempts thus far have been futile.
I'm at a standstill,
But I'm frantic.
I'm backtracking,
And rummaging through our old lives.
I'm trying to make sense of this,
Still trying to find that fucking lie.
I thought I was loving you well,
But now, I'm not sure if I was loving you at all.
I thought I was encouraging you to be the best version of yourself because I knew you deserved to finally feel empowered.
I thought I wanted the best for you because I could see how you kept yourself stuck.
But was I just trying to change you into someone you're not?
The potential I saw in you.
Instead of loving you,
simply for,

being you?

A LIFE THAT IS GONE

I'm holding on to a life that is gone.
I know this now.
I need to allow myself to become present in the new reality I find myself in.
The version of us that was never part of the plan.
The version of us where you don't love me the way that you once did,
and if I am honest,
the same goes for me, too.
I can see it in your eyes,
You once called me an angel,
and I swear you believed you were the luckiest man in the world to have found yourself by my side.
Well,
You don't look at me the same way, these days.
I was never an angel,
But I know I am more than the reflection I see of myself in your eyes.
What was it that caused my halo to fall?
Did my growth scare you?
Am I no longer deserving of my wings because I'm too unconventional for you?
Do I test you too much?
Am *I* too much?

IS THIS WORTH IT

You don't show an interest in me anymore.
My insides scream at me,
And they scream at you too.
Show me something.
Show me there is still life left in this decaying relationship.
Show me that this is still worth fighting for.
This yearning is tormenting.
Don't you see what you're doing to me?
I need you to realize that this is hurting me too.
When did this become all about you?
Do you care anymore?
Because it doesn't seem like you do.
From where I am standing,
Our once happy home has been gutted,
and we're left tiptoeing around the shell of the memories that once were.
I am lost.
And I am broken.
I need you to help me see a way out of this mess.
I want to hang the pictures back up on the walls.
I want the house to sing with warmth once more.
I want this to be a home again.
But I only make up one half of this relationship.
I can't do the work of two.
I need you to come on board,
I need you to want to mend this too.

NOSTALGIA

I don't want it to be over.
I see glimpses of my future husband,
and I truly want the world with him.
I catch him for a moment on a warm summer night,
Glowing under the sweet oranges that ignite during golden hour.
In that moment, he is nothing short of perfection.
He doesn't even know that I'm watching.
Somehow, the darkness that has engulfed us recently seems to have disappeared.
Along with my recollection of the torment I've been enduring of late.
Tonight, I want to walk over to him and tell him that I love him.
Tell him that I'm sorry for this horrible mess.
And then maybe I would forgive him,
If the sky stayed this way for long enough.
If he kept smiling at me like that.
If he welcomed me with those loving arms that I used to know so well.
I realise, these moments make me weak.
They give me feelings of nostalgia,
Made more obvious by the growing lump in my throat and the tears gently trickling from my eyes.
I wish I could have this all the time.

What I would do to make a home in this moment.

SIGNS

It's woven throughout the songs of the moment,
And the way I find comfort in old lyrics, and poetry.
It's in the arbitrary posts that appear when I start to question myself,
and it lingers cautiously in **bold** on the tip of my tongue.
These signs have been shouting at you for years now,
I start to wonder if they'll ever penetrate.
It saddens me to consider the obviousness of it all.
Could you truly be this ignorant?
The decay must be clear to you now.
Do you find comfort in this gentle death too?
Tell me, where are we these days?
And is this place a happy one for you?

PAPERS & RINGS

He said I was too scared to leave him,
Was that a dare?
When I said yes,
what was I committing myself to?
What is the meaning of a piece of paper if he can't show me that he loves me on any other day?
What is the significance of a ring when I wake each morning and I'm reminded that it didn't change a fucking thing.

P E A C E

My tormented mind won't let me rest.
Why do I feel like this is another twisted test?
I look desperately to your eyes, in hope of another sign.
I anxiously need a reminder that you are always meant to be mine.
Why can't you see what this is doing to me?
Please wake me and tell me it was all just a dream.
I need you now more than ever, but also not at all.
Tell me how I am meant to make sense of this,
before I break down and lose it all.
My mind won't let me be with you.
and it won't let me be without.
I guess peace is just a word that I know nothing about.

WHAT DOES IT MEAN TO BE FREE

She wakes, and it's murkier than usual.
The garden that once flourished here has been overrun by weeds and it's littered with decaying wildlife.
The waterfall that once flowed with life has been dried up for months now.
The sunflowers have wilted, the dandelions have lost their petals, the trees threw away their leaves, and the sun eventually forgot to shine.
It's always dark. It's lonely. It's cold. And its forgotten.
Like an abandoned house, it's eery to be here.
You know that joy existed once, but it's obvious that this derelict space is haunted by nothing more than tortured souls.
The whispers are constant, and these days they've been more like screams.
She hopelessly wonders, 'What does it mean to be free?'
You see,
she yearns for a day where she wakes up and the sun is shining gloriously back at her, as if to say she's proud.
A day where the birds are singing love songs to each other and she can hear the steady stream of the waterfall in the distance,
A day where for once,
she has control of the voices, before they take control of her.
She looks desperately at the decay that surrounds her,
she frantically searches for a sign of life, for something to remind her that this isn't it, that things will get better.
She closes her eyes and screams, 'What does it mean to be free?'
She opens her eyes.
a faint splash of orange catches her eye in the distance.
A single wildflower blooms,
standing alone, but stronger than ever,
A sign of hope, she thought,
a sign of home.

PONDER

There is a depth where I have been, that I cannot unsee.
There is a girl, at my core, that I can no longer retrieve.
There is a version of myself, that I've had to grieve.
It scares me to ponder what it might take to finally leave.

WAITING

The pain, it was all-consuming.
And the confusion seemed to get thicker the closer I got to finally speaking up.
Why does the mind try to stop you in the exact moment you finally find the courage to stand up for yourself?
For weeks, I had contemplated this delivery,
And for years, I had considered this trajectory.
The day was much the same as any other,
I was consumed by futile attempts to quiet my restless mind.
Wasted efforts trying to stop the self-sabotage and convince myself that I'm being dramatic.
Again.
He was talking about children, *gleefully*.
And although I was sitting right next to him,
I was watching us from across the room.
Disbelief.
How could he be talking about children at a time like this?
How could he be cheerfully discussing our future together whilst my mind has been consumed by nothing but thoughts of separation?
How could we be experiencing life together,
and be on entirely different pages?
I don't recall how, and I don't recall why,
But the words came stumbling out of me.
He wasn't surprised by my admission,
but I was,
because it seemed like he had been waiting to hear those words for a lifetime.

M A P S

Do you remember who you were before you met me?
Are you trying desperately to pick up the remnants of your shattered heart in hopes that they direct you safely back home,
To the person you once were.
To the person I once fell in love with.
Tell me, can you find him anymore?
I ask because I can no longer find myself.
And the truth is I'm not sure I want to.
To find her feels safe,
But how could I be her again after all this time.
She got me here,
and I'm proud of her for that,
but she doesn't *belong* here.

I seek the map that leads me to the next version of myself.
This in-between is torturous, it's dark, and it's lonely.
These days,
I'm not sure if I'm going backwards or forwards anymore.
In fact,
I realise,
I don't know anything anymore.

CORPSE

I feel like a decaying corpse.
I've been abandoned but how can that be true if it was all my own undoing?
I imagine there are still evident pieces of myself that remain,
Sections that haven't yet started to rot.
Perhaps they symbolize my foundations,
The parts of myself that were always me,
Even before I became everyone else.
Maybe, it's the freckle that remains on my finger, despite the loss of the ring that sparkled perfectly next to it.
Maybe it's the scar that sits upon my left knee, reminding me to be free.
No.
It's more obvious than that.
My hair, brown, and though it's become dull, it remains in the high bun I always wear,
Or my eyes, green, and open, but desperately wanting to close.
I feel hollow,
which feels like a contradiction.
I worry that things will only get worse,
that there is still more of me that I need to let go of.
I'm not sure that I can handle that yet,
And I'm not sure how I can prepare myself for that.

HURTING MYSELF

I'm left with more space than I know how to handle.
And that makes me feel pathetic.
I don't want to deal with this anymore,
mostly because I don't know how to.
I'm spiralling again,
And I'm scared of myself.
I don't know what I'm supposed to do.
I want your shoulder to cry on,
and I want your arms around me.
but I know that I can't have either.
Why did I do this to myself?
The most tragic part of it all is that there's no going back,
There doesn't get to be a do over,
How the fuck am I meant to live like this?
Everything feels empty and I don't know how I'm supposed to fill it.
I'm struggling, and I hate myself for that.
I don't know how to stop myself from hurting myself.

DO YOU DREAM

I wonder,
do you dream?
Was there ever a vision you had for yourself,
And please,
be honest,
did it ever include me?

WARNING

What they forget to tell you is that the more you awaken within yourself,
The more you learn about your patterns,
your limiting beliefs,
your triggers,
and all the ways you keep yourself small,
The less capable you are of taking it all back.
Of unseeing it.
How can you possibly lie to yourself now that you've gained a whole new perspective?
Sure, you can do your best to ignore your intuition,
You can choose to refuse to answer the call of your soul.
But that road is a treacherous one too.
What they forget to tell you is that,
Whatever you decide,
It will hurt,
If you choose to listen,
or you choose to ignore,
it will fucking hurt.
And I just wish someone could have warned me about that.

I'M NOT DEAD

I'm in a state of continual rumination,
I'm held like a prisoner lost in a trance.
I've contained my world to the replays that exist in my head,
and the conversations I have trying to convince myself that
I'm not dead.

CATALYST

Was my role in all of this to be the catalyst,
Or am I giving myself too much credit.
Maybe I'm just a pessimist looking for a way to make herself the victim.
Being the protagonist never looked good on me anyway,
Theres a growing list of people who can reassure you of that.

BLACK DUCK COURT

There's a piece of me who will live on in these four walls.
She's from another timeline, a life I no longer choose.
I find comfort in knowing that she will be here,
In my first home,
with my first love,
living my first life.
It saddens me deeply to leave, it's an ache I haven't found the words yet to describe,
How can I take all of this with me?
How do I say goodbye to the life that I dreamed of ever since I was a little girl?
How do I accept that I got everything I wanted but it was never meant for me?
There is a part of me that wishes I could have stayed here forever,
Had I not questioned my reality.
Had I not yearned for more,
We could have stayed,
We could have been happy,
We could have had forever,
here,
at Black Duck Court.

L I E S

I told you nothing changes,
But I lied,
Because everything does.
I told you we could still be friends,
But friends aren't meant to hurt each other like this.
I had the best of intentions,
But I couldn't foresee this pain.
How can nothing change,
When I no longer look at you the same.
The version of who I thought you were,
Is unravelling at a rapid rate.
I'm seeing you clearly for the first time,
and it's becoming far too much for me to take.
I told you nothing changes,
But I lied,
Because everything does.

YOU SAID NOTHING

He said to take the emotion out of it,
Like it wasn't my entire life collapsing in front of me
Like I wasn't losing complete control over the life I had envisioned for myself
Like I wasn't enduring the worst months of my life
Like I wasn't saying goodbye to everything I had ever known
Like I wasn't holding on for dear life
Like I wasn't breaking my own heart
And watching
As you sat there
And said nothing.

SURFACE LOVE

I held on for far too long, I can see that now.
I was prepared to sacrifice every ounce of my being to make this work,
But you never saw that, did you?
I was ready to take ownership of all our mistakes,
I was willing to take the fall if it meant that we could work this out.
If it meant that I got my ending.
I see now, this life wasn't meant for me.
And it wasn't meant for you either.
But you knew that too, didn't you?
I get lost in curious thoughts about you.
I lose chunks of time trying to piece together your mind, in attempt to bring me closure.
I understand why I held on for so long,
But I cannot seem to fathom why you did.
Why watch me dismantle myself, just to keep the peace?
Why torment yourself, trying to be someone you never wanted to be?
And why spend eight years of your life only ever loving someone on the surface?

REPRESSION

I'm finished with this repression.
I bet you loved how I played my role as the good girl.
Keeping you comfortable while my insides burned,
And my mind ate itself from the inside out.
You would rather watch my undoing,
Then do anything to disrupt your own comfort.
I think I'm angrier at myself now.
You gave me no reason to give you the benefit of the doubt,
But I did every time.
Maybe it was me who was afraid of growth,
Maybe it was me who was afraid of change.

I N H A L E

It's eerie because it's calm.
The birds are singing love songs outside,
and that feels poetic considering it's Valentine's Day.
I feel like I can finally let go,
There's nothing more I can do in this moment.
The storm has come through,
And it has torn my soul to shreds.
Somehow, I'm still standing.
Somehow, I'm still here.
I sit in silence,
listening only to the birds.
I notice that my mind is finally quiet,
I inhale like it's the first time I've taken in air in years.

A POETS DARE

The poets dared me to dream,
They insisted that there was more to my reality than I could have ever imagined.
They reminded me of the possibilities that exist outside of this world I had settled for.
But what if I'm not yet ready to hold the things that they promised to me?

N E V E R

I hope you never have to know how it feels to cry silently next to the person who is meant to love you the most because you've learned that it's easier to console yourself than it is to explain your pain to a person who is not willing to understand you.

I hope you never have to know what it feels like to watch them fall out of love with you, agonising over every detail, every minute action, or inaction, wondering what else you could do, or what more it might take.

And I truly hope you never waste years of your life wondering why the person you considered your world, was never capable of seeing you at all.

THE OBVIOUS

It still catches me off guard sometimes,
the obviousness of it all.
How easily this could have all been mended,
Had you seen how my yearnings were never meant to be grand compromises,
Or how my longings were never meant to be impossible responsibilities.
My love,
I was never setting you up only to watch you fail.

CHECKPOINT

This feels like a checkpoint of sorts.
A new point to remind me that I can never go back,
that I reset from here now.
More distance has inched its way between us,
And even more unknowns are yet to be faced.
Three months somehow feels like three days and three years,
All at once.
Is this what they mean by shifting timelines?
The girl I was three months ago barely resembles the
shadows of who I am today.
It makes me wonder; do you feel different too?
In another life, this would have been our wedding day.
In a different timeline, we would have said 'I do'.

HOW?

How do I tell my mother that I'm finding it harder and harder to hold on?
How do I tell her that I can't breathe even though there is air still filling my lungs?
How do I tell her that this agony that she cannot see, is slowly killing me?
How do I tell her that it's getting harder to wake up every morning, and even harder to look at myself in the mirror?
How do I tell her that I don't recognise myself anymore, and that I have this desperate desire to escape the confines of my very skin?
How do I tell her that I've ran out of ways to convince myself to get up off the floor?
But mostly, how do I tell my mother that this fight was over long before I tried to find the words to tell her?

RIOT

There is a weight resting fragilely along the shelf of my shoulder blades,
How can something invisible cause such a riot?

DWINDLING OPTIONS

We sit,
And we're nearly seated in the same positions we sat when we ended our relationship three short months ago.
A peculiar parallel.
You notice my distance and ask me cautiously what's going through my mind.
I ponder that question,
Perhaps for a moment too long.
You can see my mind strategically selecting my next words.
How do I tell you that all I can hear are defeated whispers directing me to end my life?
How do I tell you that these pleas are convincing me that my options are dwindling?
I want to tell you.
But it feels too heavy.
So,
I avoid your gaze,
and I convince you that I'm overwhelmed.
You comfort me with niceties,
And you tell me you understand.
I get lost in a daydream,
Wishing myself out of my skin.
And as usual,
You don't suspect a thing.

BARE BONES

I have an intense impulse to throw away everything I've ever owned.
Shove it in a bag and never look back, never think twice.
It doesn't feel right to bring it with me to my next life.
I worry that I don't have what it takes to face the bare bones that will remain when that task is complete.
Can I see myself, really? Can I face that reality?
Everything feels like I lie these days,
I look at myself and I feel like a stranger,
I'm different somehow, but I'm yet to pinpoint where exactly that change resides within me.
It's complicated, nothing fits right, and nothing feels right.
And now I'm wondering if it ever did.
Time has suspended me in this space in-between.
A place I've been lingering in for weeks now.
It hasn't gotten easier.
I haven't been able to find a temporary home here.
I haven't found ease in this standstill.
I look around at this half-emptied home and I can see the newness that is desperate to create permanency in my life.
I cling to the moments where I catch myself imagining them in my next home,
It's the only glimpse of hope I encounter these days.

TREES

Something has changed within me,
I feel lighter.
The sun is out, its warm, but it's not unpleasant.
There's something magical about days like these.
The peace is different.
The sun is shining easily through the white sheer curtains,
and there's a gentle breeze.
I can hear the slight rustle of the leaves falling from the tree
that resides in the front yard.
It's Autumn, and the leaves are slowly losing their greenery,
they started to fall earlier than usual this year.
I read once that the trees can help heal you.
And when I see this tree on days like today,
I am convinced that they do.
I learned that their roots are all connected underground,
and they heal each other when one is lacking.
I've heard that they remember you, too.
When we bought this house four years ago,
the tree was half this size.
I would get bothered by the mess it made during Autumn,
I used to think it was such a nuisance.
Something is different now.
Soon, this tree won't be in my front yard.
Soon, I'll need to leave,
and this tree won't be here to help me heal.

HAD I KNOWN

Had I known back then that the decision I was about to make
would be the one to lead me to more pain,
Would I have made the same detrimental decision?
Would I have chosen to stay instead?

TRUST

I'm sitting outside in the middle of the night while I wait for some courage to overcome me and I finally free myself of the last tether that attaches me to my previous life.
I pull my legs into my chest,
I tip my head back slightly and close my eyes.
I allow my mind to wander.
And when I do,
I can feel your arms around me,
Though I don't yet know who you are.
We're somewhere far from home,
But it doesn't feel unsafe,
it never is when I'm with you.
I'm wrapped in a blanket,
As well as your arms,
the nights have started to cool,
Winter is coming.
I lean back against your chest,
As we sit under an open sky,
The waves are crashing carefully,
and the stars are shining magically.
We talk about our previous lives and laugh at the thought that at one point in time, we didn't know the other existed.
We silently consider how unfathomable that feels now.
We talk about all the paths that lead us to this moment.
To this place, here with each other.
Finally, after all this time

BALANCE

I contemplate this theory around balance,
I consider yin and yang.
I've heard that when a door closes,
the other will finally open.
I've learned that deep suffering goes hand in hand with profound pleasure.
Some days, this concept brings me hope.
It reminds me that this grief, it won't have been for nothing,
That I didn't throw everything away, only to be rewarded with loneliness.
But I fear that the best of my journey has already been experienced,
And this excruciating grief, it's here to balance the scale.

OLD FRIENDS

It's hard to envision old friends making new memories without me.
A repercussion from a decision I made some time ago.
Picturing them out to dinner,
Sharing new stories and laughing about jokes I won't get to understand.
It hurts to know that at some point in time, these were my people,
and at some point in time, I would have been there,
with them,
at that table.
I feel like a ghost haunting my previous life.
Clutching on to any trace of my former self,
Desperately hoping it settles me with comfort and helps me to pretend that my life isn't falling to pieces around me.
I wonder if I still cross their mind.
I wonder if they catch themselves glancing around the table when the waiter asks if they want any more drinks.
Do they remember that there used to be another?
Or is it possible that they don't think of me at all?

STRINGS

The end is inching its way closer,
I've been slowly removing the remaining strings that tie me to you, and the life we thought we would share together.
The more that I let go,
The tighter I want to hold on to everything that remains.
The more that I release,
the closer I get to having to face myself.
How on earth do I do that?
I realise now that I've been removing the distractions,
I've been peeling back the layers and learning which parts of myself are aligned with the version of me I am today,
and which parts are here because of external influence.
I become anxious when I consider the removal of the final string,
will I be left with anything at all?
My life was weaved so generously into yours,
and I'm not sure if a whole human will be here when this is over.
How did I allow myself to get so entangled in another?
And how do I ensure that I don't ever allow myself to do it again?

THE ONE AFTER ME

I don't want to know what she looks like,
Or if there are traces of me, scattered within her.
I don't want to be compared,
And I don't want to be reassured.
I would be lying if I said it didn't hurt,
Of course, it fucking hurts.
How did you manage to weave your words to find a fleeting moment?
In what scenario are you not consumed by the decay of your previous life that you had it in you to begin anew with another?
Already.
I think the part that consumes me the most,
Is how quickly our paths have drifted,
And the stark reality of how easily replaceable I really was to you.

UNCLAIMED WORDS

There are unclaimed words that exist somewhere in the universe because he wasn't ready to hold them.
Can I salvage them somehow?
Can I keep them safe until I find someone who is willing to hold them?

BLISS

I'm convinced there will come a day where I don't need to talk about him.
I'm sure the fact that I don't think of him will be a strange realisation considering he was my entire world for a time.
But for now, he still lingers.
For now, he clings to my fingertips.
He's the dull pulse that generally goes unnoticed.
He's the catching on clothes when your hands are dry.
I'm slowly shedding the remnants of him,
And as more distance is created,
I can feel myself becoming lighter.
And let me tell you,
it's bliss.

P R O U D

Today, I told myself that I was proud.
It took courage to dismantle my belief system.
It was brave to destroy the vision I clung to.
And it took guts to trust in the rebuild.

TWO KIDS

We were just two kids who saw each other and something about it felt like home.
We weren't to know that we were worlds apart,
no one teaches you that lasting love requires a level of depth we wouldn't have the means to get to.
I know people change,
some more than others,
and others not at all.
We were just two kids,
We weren't to know.

THE PRESENT

There are parts of me that want to uncover every mystery
until I can finally make sense of it all.
They want to travel through all my memories, all the albums,
and all our messages to pinpoint where it all went wrong,
And attempt to comprehend when I decided that I deserved
this, and when he decided to give up on it all.
I want to uncover all the unspoken words,
and the subtle changes in behaviour.
Because I still have unanswered questions.
Though, I realise now they're mostly for myself.
And if I truly want to answer them,
it would mean I would need to make a home in my past.
To delve deeply into our former selves would require the
death of the life I have ahead of me.
I won't do it again.
I thought that by revisiting the past,
facing the hard truths, and honouring my emotions,
It would help to ease my withered soul.
I thought it would fast track this healing journey,
And I thought it would help me grow.
In many ways it has,
but it's simultaneously created more havoc,
And more pain.
This time, I'll keep the albums on the shelf.
This time, I choose the present.

THE HATRED I HARBOUR

It's been a long week,
But then, maybe it's been longer.
Each day has been fuelled with vile self-talk and an inability to look directly at my reflection.
I hate myself.
Another day has passed and it's getting harder to ignore the repulsive slurs coming from within.
I try to ignore them,
maybe I can convince myself that it's just my cycle, again.
My patience is dwindling,
and today, the battle is finally lost.
After dinner, my fingers have found their way forcefully down my throat,
I ignore the inner voice that is pleading with me to stop.
It's been years since I've found myself here,
and although it's obvious that I am losing control,
I'm simultaneously reclaiming it.
I am desperate.
There's an urgency to undo all the things I've done today, yesterday, this whole week.
Why do I feel more whole when there is less of me?
I try to remember to be kind; I attempt to remind myself of the pain I've been through.
I hopelessly ask myself to find compassion instead of contributing to my own suffering.
I'm unsuccessful.
Tomorrow, I'll wake with a raw throat and a dull headache.
Both subtle reminders of the hatred I'm harbouring for myself.
And then,
we start again.

LEAP OF FAITH

Why is the prospect of death more alluring than facing the discomfort that comes with the unknown?
I'm free falling out of my old life,
I'm plummeting at a rate that is too fast for my heart to take.
Everything is unknown,
and I wish I could be excited about that,
but I hate feeling like I'm losing control.
I've never been free enough to find comfort in change.
I don't know how to move forward into a life I've never known.
How can I take the first step when I can't see the ground below me?
How can I trust myself to move in the right direction when I've never taken a leap of faith before?

MY PUTRID PORTRAIT

I can see the rage glistening cautiously in her eyes,
Her red stained teeth doing their best to mask those insidious slurs.
How long had she been waiting to free herself of these words?
And was she flooded with regret or relief after they fell easily from her drunken lips?
She can rest comfortably surrounded by this pile of lies,
She can go on believing that every one of them is mine.
I'll let her paint this putrid portrait of me,
Make it ugly,
And make it mean,
But most of all,
make it anything but me.

THIS STEADY REBUILD

When I scream, there are still echoes.
A stark reminder, that I am still empty.
It's an exhausting venture, this steady rebuild.

LOOPS

She explained that these places hold old energies,
And they're doing their best to keep me stuck.
These loops play out without regard,
Reminding me only of what has been lost.
She said it's up to me to change the narrative,
to find new meaning, and new light.
And if that isn't possible,
I need to consider leaving these places in the past forever.
Accepting that, perhaps that is where they belong.

TEACHINGS

How can I teach my hands to hold me when they've only ever known of the importance to hold another.
How can I convince my heart that I will keep her safe when I've never proven myself trustworthy before.
And how do I show my mind that I won't allow it to spiral again, so that it can finally rest.

THE STARS

When I sit beneath the stars,
I am reminded of my insignificance.
My perspective is shattered,
And then gently placed back into focus.
I watch the stillness of the night sky,
And I finally feel at peace.
I consider the worlds that exist beyond this one,
And suddenly my tears don't feel as necessary.
I sit in awe as I contemplate my existence,
I try to remember why I came outside in the first place.
I begin to dry my tears,
And I realise the stars ground me in ways you never could.

THIS IMPOSSIBLE QUEST

I wonder if I'll ever get complete closure.
I wonder if I'll ever get answers to my questions,
or if I'll eventually get tired,
or distracted,
and finally give up on this impossible quest.
My mind has wandered along many paths to find answers to the questions I won't ever be able to ask.
I've found some answers hidden in plain sight,
And others have come to me through new connections,
and new conversations.
But there's one question I still find myself wanting to ask.
It's one that only you can answer.

Why was it so hard to love me?

FOUNDATIONS

I learned that my foundations were non-existent,
And that I played my role as chameleon effortlessly because there wasn't any part of me that was genuinely authentic.
I learned that to exist in a world where I do not become intertwined with another,
would mean that I needed to build new structures that will knowingly be shaken by others,
but will not be destroyed in the wake of their leave.
This is where I am now.
I'm taking this winter,
I'm intentionally rebuilding my foundations.
I know that people will come,
and I know that they will go,
This time, it will be different.
This time, I know my foundations won't fall.

SOFTLY SPOKEN SUBTLETIES

I recognise the feeling that I am experiencing now.
It's triggered by the sensation of being in the in between.
Like I'm still in this season,
also, stuck in the last,
and somehow slowly moving toward the next.
It's when I begin to feel uncomfortable in all the places that were once comfortable.
I know it's time to leap.
To trust that there's something new waiting,
and it's better than the place that I'm currently lingering in.
But how can I know when it's the right time to jump?
And what am I meant to jump toward?
Awareness is complicated because you can't unlearn it.
You can try to ignore your intuition,
You can attempt to live in delusion,
But the nags will always be there,
Manifesting as softly spoken subtleties,
And quiet whispers in the night,
It will always find a way to remind you that there is much more to life than what you're settling for.

THIS DREADFUL PLACE

I'm contemplating all the ways I could die today,
If only I were courageous enough to go through with it.
If only I could find a way to turn the wheel at the right moment,
Or pick up my sharpest blade without hesitating.
But that's just it,
isn't it.
I'm not courageous.
I'm nothing more than a fraud.
I'm inspired, but not inspired enough to leap.
I'm tired of this life, but not tired enough to leave it.
I'm exhausted by my mind but not exhausted enough to put an end to it.
I need someone to help me to find a way to leave this dreadful place.

A SINKING SHIP

It's a sinking ship,
The size of my heart.
We're not taught that when you abandon your home,
You don't get to go back and save it when the fires come
through to claim it.
And so,
I keep a safe distance,
to avoid any confusion,
to avoid making this harder.
I watch as you sink further,
Knowing that I can't be your lifeboat anymore.

LUCK

She said that I was lucky.
I find myself surrounded by endless opportunities,
I have abundant options,
I have the freedom to take my next step without considering how it affects anyone else.
And so, I agreed without hesitation.
But then I remembered the bravery it took to get me here.
The courage it took to remove myself from the only life I had ever envisioned.
It wasn't luck that got me here,
It was the compilation of hard decisions,
Leaps of faith,
And a deep trust that the discomfort would be worth it.
That this was all leading me to a place that was more aligned.
To a version of me that was more authentic.
And to a life that I wholeheartedly decided to pursue.
I am not lucky,
I created this life for myself.

CLOSED DOORS

When I catch myself talking about him now,
Its fleeting, almost without a second thought.
His name no longer breaks as it falls from my mouth.
And their eyes no longer dart when I mention my past.
It's become a fond, and distant memory,
Like I'm talking about an old friend.
Is this how I know the door is finally closed?

EMMA

Where would I be had I not found a friend in you?
This journey has been one full of unexpected turns,
And unpredictable pain.
This path has weathered me with more heartache than one human is capable of handling.
My mind has trekked through to eery places
and forbidden corners that I could never have known existed.
And you,
As you do,
graciously walked the weary road alongside me.
Without hesitation,
and without question.
Do you know that you became my rock?
You are the lighthouse on the edge of my wild ocean,
Reminding me that the shore is this way,
Should I ever get lost in the depths of my own chaos.
You are the gentle moon, elegantly lighting my night sky,
Reminding me that there is a place for our darkness to be held and cherished,
And that I don't need to hide these parts of myself to be beautiful.
Platonic love is something that doesn't get enough credit.
You have been my safe place, my supporter, and my soul sister.
Thank you for your gentle redirections, your subtle reminders, and your endless love.
You truly are a precious soul.

STABLE FOUNDATION

I miss the security of a stable foundation.
Of a path not set in stone,
but loosely laid ahead with an option to veer if I so desired.
I used to be sure of what I wanted,
Of where I wanted to go,
Of whom I wanted to be.
Nowadays, I feel aloof.
And most days, my life doesn't feel real.
I've created this temporary theme that rules over my current existence,
This is still the in-between,
It just looks different.

ON MY HARDEST DAYS

On my hardest days,
I would tell you to stay where you are.
I would tell you it's not worth the inner turmoil.
It's not worth constantly reassuring yourself that choosing you would be worth it.
That it would be the right decision.
Today, it's not.
Today, it's lonely.
On my hardest days,
I would tell you that being somewhere that is safe is easier than constantly feeling like a fraud.
I would tell you that the comfort of the known is easier than rebuilding your life from the nothingness that remains once the dust has finally settled.
Today, everything is hard.
Today, I hate myself for the decisions I made.
On my hardest days,
I would tell you that I come close to regret.
I would tell you that the mental battle is just as constant on this side of the fence.
But even on my hardest days,
I know,
I would tell you,
I could have never stayed.

SAFE PLACES

It served me as a cocoon.
A safe place where I could hide in the shadows while I allowed time to heal my tender wounds.
A place that protected me,
as I patiently regained my strength,
and it allowed me to exist in peace while I delicately began to rebuild myself.
Away from the outside world,
Away from the darkness.
It permitted me to sit with myself in solitude.
It was akin to a warm embrace,
And a tall and sturdy wall,
The ultimate protection that allowed me to take the time I needed to be still,
To rebuild,
And now,
It is demanding that I spread my wings,
and soar.

MY NEW BEGINNING

There is a fondness that accompanies my memories of him,
and us,
and the life we once shared.
The bitterness has gone, I mean that, truly.
As has the anxiety that used to penetrate my being when I considered the lost trajectory.
They will all politely tell you,
'It just takes time'.
And this isn't far from the truth.
But this journey demanded much more from me than my time.
It asked me to grieve a future I saw for myself,
It asked me to let go of people and places I never imagined myself living without,
It invited me to be alone,
to discover who I was now,
without him by my side.
Perhaps the hardest demand of all?
It asked me to be born,
And then it ordered me to die,
Many times over,
To grieve that life,
And that version of me,
to make way for my new beginning.

TO YOU, DEAR READER

I write this message to you, dear Reader.
I encourage you to stay vulnerable,
And to remain open to the magic of this world.
Life is hard, it will weather you,
your soul will break a million times over and you will wonder if this fight is worth it.
I want you to know that it is,
Fighting for yourself will always be worth it.
No one else can convince you of this,
but I hope one day you truly believe that you are meant to be here.
You are meant to take up space in some little corner on this earth,
That space is yours.
I dare you to fill it.
I challenge you to hold it.
I encourage you to claim it.
The world needs what you have to offer,
People need your light.
Please, go and embrace all you are, the dark and the light, the hard and the soft, the broken and the strong.
You are human, after all, you are not meant to be perfect.
Hold all that you are,
Never forget your value.
Never forget to shine your uniqueness onto this earth,
The world will thank you for it,
But mostly,
you will thank yourself for it.

CLOSURE

When I began working on this collection, I hoped that it would lead to some version of acceptance. I hoped I could move through the grief and the torment, and I hoped that I would eventually find peace.

If you've made it this far, I would like to thank you for taking the time to get lost in my past with me.

It's been over a year now as I write this message. And when I read back on this collection, I'm in awe of how far I've come.

If you're struggling with grief of some sort, whether that be a friend, a family member, a lover, a pet, or an old version of yourself. Please don't give up, and please don't lose hope. You will find yourself again, and your life will come together in new and more aligned ways, and one day, you will look back and be inspired by those younger versions of you who helped see you through it.

Today, I am at peace with this phase of my life. Though I couldn't have fathomed it at the time, the version of myself that lives on within these pages represents only a chapter of my life. These thoughts no longer consume me, and this chapter no longer defines me.

Change has been one of the hardest challenges for me to move through and get comfortable with. The unsteadiness, the upheaval, the unease. But without it, I wouldn't have found this version of me, and I wouldn't be who I am or where I am today.

If the dragonfly finds you, whether that be today, four months from now, or in ten years. I hope that it's a comforting sign. I hope you can find it in you to embrace the challenges it will bring, knowing that it will be hard, and it will be ugly, but it will be so very worth it.

With love,
Makaila x

www.ingramcontent.com/pod-product-compliance
Lightning Source LLC
Chambersburg PA
CBHW070333120526
44590CB00017B/2866